Castles _and_ cathedrals

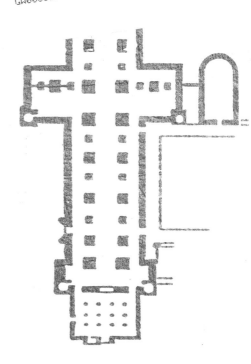

PATRICIA DAWSON _and_ IAN DAWSON

Oxford University Press 1992

🔖 Acknowledgments

The publishers would like to thank the following for permission to reproduce photographs:
Aerofilms p 16 (bottom); Associated Press p 47 (top); Bayeux (Tapisserie de Bayeux et avec autorisation spécial de la Ville de Bayeux) p 44; Bibliotheque Nationale p 7 (bottom left); Bridgeman Art Library p 14, p 17 (bottom left); British Library p 7 (top), p 16 (top), p 18; English Heritage p 6 (top), p 12–13 (bottom), p 27 (bottom), p 29 (centre), p 39 (bottom); E.T. Archive p 28 (top), p 33 (top), p 39 (bottom); Fotomas Index p 31; Michael Holford p 7 (bottom right), p 8, p 10, p 12 (left), p 28 (left & bottom), p 29 (bottom), p 33 (bottom), p 36; A. F. Kersting p 6 (bottom left), p 27 (top left), p 29 (top); Public Record Office p 5 (centre); Royal Commission on the Historical Monuments of England p 5 (top), p 17 (top right), p 21; Skyscan Aerial Photography p 12–13 (top), p 39 (top); Syndication International p 6 (bottom right); The Boad of Trinity College Dublin p 17 (top left); Woodmansterne p 26, p 27 (top right), p 47 (bottom); York Minster Archives p 17 (bottom right)

Cover: British Library

Illustrations: Christopher Chaisty: p 8, p 15–16, p 20, p 26, p 34, p 37, p 43; Martin Cottam: p 3–4, p 9–10, p 45–46; Simon Evans: p 22–24, p 36, p 40–41; Anthony Knill: p 9, p 11, p 38; Fiona Powers: p 15, p 25, p 29, p 43

Maps and diagrams: Oxford Illustrators

Preface

This book is an investigation into life in the Middle Ages, using castles and cathedrals jointly as evidence. The introduction establishes a general question: 'What was life like in the Middle Ages?' and also four, more specific, sub-questions, each of which is the focus for one of the succeeding chapters. On pages 6–7 pupils are invited to suggest initial answers or hypotheses in response to these questions, using the material in the introduction and their existing ideas, assumptions or prejudices. These first ideas from groups or individuals should be recorded (in pupils' books or as a wall-display) and then developed when pupils have undertaken fieldwork and worked on the material in each chapter. A later comparison between the initial answers and the final conclusions should boost pupils' confidence by helping them appreciate how much they have learned about the way castles and cathedrals help us to understand life in the Middle Ages.

The book has been designed to support and complement fieldwork. Experience has shown that pupils gain the most from fieldwork by visiting a site or sites at the beginning of a course, seeking evidence to answer questions. Hence the natural timing of fieldwork in relation to this book would be after the introduction and before Chapter 1. This would allow pupils to a) suggest answers to questions using the introductory material; b) develop or amend these answers as a result of the site visit(s), and c) further develop their answers after working on each chapter. Pupils will be able to use the combined material on castles and cathedrals even if they have not visited both kinds of sites. There is no necessity for pupils to learn a detailed outline of architectural development before undertaking fieldwork. This knowledge is more effectively acquired as the investigation proceeds (see particularly chapter 4). Pictures of castles and cathedrals for sequencing and duration activities are included in the accompanying Resource Package.

This book can also be used to complement *Medieval Realms* in this series. *Medieval Realms* is an investigation into the degree of change in the Middle Ages and *Castles and Cathedrals* can be used as a case-study to test the conclusions reached in *Medieval Realms*. If using *Castles and Cathedrals* as a case-study, teachers may choose to investigate only some of the questions in this book or divide the questions amongst pupils, with different groups of pupils working on each of the four chapters.

Opportunities for recording pupils' work in relation to Attainment Targets are provided in the exercises indicated by the headings in the chart on page 48. Further Homework Sheets linked to Attainment Targets can be found in the Resource Package. Last but not least, we hope that the stories that open and close the book are enjoyable. At the very least they should act as a reminder that castles were once full of life and homes for people very like us — they were not built as ruins!

Patricia Dawson   Ian Dawson

Introduction

▨ Accident!

The children stood and blinked in the sunlight. It was dark and smoky in their home, but outside the sun was shining brightly. The boy, Leofwin, turned as his father came out behind him. Leofwin was cross. 'We'll not manage it, father. Not just me and Gudrun. We can't finish the harvest on our own.'

'But you'll have to, son', his father replied. 'It's sunny enough now but those clouds are bringing rain. If we don't get the barley in, and dried, we'll all be hungry before the winter's out.'

Then Gudrun joined in. 'Tell the Normans you can't help them. Tell them our harvest is more important than their castle. Tell them to go away and leave us alone. They don't even talk like us.'

But by now their father was walking down towards the river. 'What good would that do? The Normans are here, and here to stay. They want men to unload stone from the barges for their precious castle so I've no choice. I have to go and so must you. Your mother will take over from you as soon as she can.' So Leofwin shrugged his shoulders, shouted goodbye and headed for the fields, carrying the scythe.

Their mother stood in the doorway of the hut, holding bread and apples for the children's lunch. Gudrun wrapped the food in a cloth and ran after her brother. They soon got to work alongside the older villagers who were not needed by the Normans. Leofwin cut the barley and Gudrun bundled it up.

Leofwin tried to copy the old man next to them by swinging the scythe in an easy circle. At first he worked quickly but, as the morning passed, he grew tired. His back hurt and his shoulders ached. He hated the barley — he even hated the sunshine — but most of all he hated the Normans. As he moved slowly across the field he muttered and swore.

Gudrun could see that Leofwin was tired. 'Let me have a go with the scythe', she said 'while you have an apple'. As he looked up, Leofwin let the scythe swing round. It caught him on the leg. He saw the blood spurt out and then he felt the pain. He fell to the ground, screaming.

Gudrun grabbed the lunch cloth, scattering the bread and apples amongst the barley. She wrapped the cloth round his leg, tying it tightly. 'This is what mother did when you fell against the cart wheel', she said. 'I hope it's the right thing to do. You must keep still.' But Leofwin wasn't listening; he was shouting and crying and calling for his father.

Leofwin was far too heavy for Gudrun to carry home. 'I'm going for help', she said. 'Old Swithin's coming. He'll stay with you till I get back. I'm going to get father.' She hooked up her long skirt and held it in one hand as she ran across the fields. She could still hear Leofwin crying as she turned down the hill towards the river.

At first she couldn't see her father. All the fit men from the village were there with the Norman soldiers, trying to get the stone blocks from the barges. Then she saw him, harnessing the ox pair to the cart. Straightaway he knew there was trouble. 'What is it, Gudrun? Where's Leo?' He started to run towards the fields, almost before she had answered.

By the time Gudrun had got back up the hill, Leofwin had stopped crying and Father was re-tying the cloth. 'You did the right thing there', he said. 'It's lucky that you knew what to do. There's a lot of blood, but it's not a deep cut. He'll be up and running in a few days.' He scooped Leofwin up into his arms and carried the boy home.

Leofwin's father was right. Leofwin wasn't an invalid for long, but his leg took a long time to heal completely. So that was another thing his family blamed the Normans for. The soldiers had taken good farming land for their castle. They made the village men help build the castle, and now Leofwin's leg was injured. In the nearby town a new bishop was changing services in the cathedral. The villagers longed for the Normans to go away and leave them in peace, just like it was in the old days.

☷ Finding out about life in the Middle Ages

Source A

The remains of a medieval house, excavated by archaeologists in the village of Wharram Percy.

Is the story true?

We do not know of a real boy called Leofwin who cut his leg badly in the year 1070, but a lot of the story *is* true. At that time, Norman soldiers were building castles and the English way of life was changing, whether the people liked it or not.

The Normans made great changes to the buildings in England. They built castles where there had never been any before. They tore down and rebuilt English cathedrals so that they were much larger. Today we can still see and visit many of these castles and cathedrals, even if some are now in ruins.

Castles and cathedrals are very important sources of evidence about life in the middle ages. In this book you will be investigating what these castles and cathedrals tell us about the lives and skills of people who lived in our towns and villages in the Middle Ages. But, before we begin, what ideas do you already have about the lives of people like Leofwin, Gudrun and their parents? Were their lives similar to, or different from, yours? Look back to the story you have just read for some clues or think about films or cartoons you have seen about life in the Middle Ages.

☷ Different kinds of sources

Castles and cathedrals are not the only sources that tell us about life in the Middle Ages, but they are particularly helpful. There may be a castle or cathedral near where you live, so you could visit it to help your investigation.

Source B

An extract from Domesday Book, a record of most towns and villages in England. The information was collected in 1086–7.

FINDING OUT ABOUT THE MIDDLE AGES

1 Look at Sources A and B. What do they tell you about life in the Middle Ages?
2 Why is it difficult for you to find out about life in the Middle Ages from Sources A and B?
3 Why might you find out more about life in the Middle Ages from castles and cathedrals than from Sources A and B?
4 What other kinds of sources might tell us about medieval life?

✺ What do castles and cathedrals tell us about medieval life?

It's now time to think about castles and cathedrals more carefully. What can they tell us about medieval life? The sources and questions on these pages will help you begin your investigation.

Source C
Restormel Castle in Cornwall was built around 1200.

Source D
Winchester Cathedral. Most of the building you can see in this picture was completed in the fourteenth century.

Source E
Caernarfon Castle in Wales, built by Edward I in 1284

USING CASTLES AND CATHEDRALS AS EVIDENCE

1 Why do you think castles and cathedrals were needed?

2 What do the sources tell us about the skills and intelligence of medieval people?

3 Do you think medieval life was very comfortable? Explain your answer.

4 Was there much change during the Middle Ages (1066–1500) or did the way people lived stay the same?

5 Now look back at your answers to questions 1–4. How would you describe life in the Middle Ages, using castles and cathedrals as your sources?

Source F

This fifteenth century illustration shows stone being quarried, perhaps for the building in the background.

Source G

A drawing of a stone mason and building labourers at work, from the 1180's.

Source H

Durham Cathedral. Most of the building you can see in this picture was completed by 1150.

Now that you've answered these questions you have begun your investigation into the way medieval people lived. Your answer to question 5 is your first rough answer or hypothesis. Next you must investigate castles and cathedrals in more detail, to see whether your initial idea — your hypothesis — is right or whether it needs revising.

Why were castles and cathedrals needed?

THEY NEEDED CATHEDRALS BECAUSE RELIGION WAS IMPORTANT...

...AND THEY NEEDED CASTLES BECAUSE THEY ENJOYED FIGHTING.

Do you agree with Joe and Seenat? Or did you have other ideas when you answered the first question on page 6? This chapter will investigate why castles and cathedrals were needed and what that tells us about the activities and interests of medieval people. Then you'll be able to check your first answer as well as Joe and Seenat's.

1066–1100: a great time for building

The Norman Conquest changed many things in England. One of the greatest changes was to buildings. Before 1066 there were hardly any castles in England but by 1100 there was a castle in every important town and in a lot of other places too. There had been cathedrals before 1066 – but the Normans simply tore down many of them and began building new ones. Why did they make these changes?

Seenat was right. The Normans did build cathedrals because they thought that religion was very important. For example, William the Conqueror started the building of Battle Abbey to give thanks to God for his victory over Harold at Hastings.

One reason for castle building was that the Normans were good at fighting and thought that it was important. Men came from far and wide to join William the Conqueror's army in 1066 because they knew he was a good commander. The Normans had castles in their own country, which they used as bases for their armies and so they built castles in England as well.

But there were other reasons why the Normans built castles and cathedrals after 1066. The questions below and the evidence on pages 8–10 will help you find out what those reasons were.

Source A

Near the beginning of the Bayeux Tapestry, William and Harold are shown as friends because they fought together against William's enemies. This was before 1066.

CAUSES AND CONSEQUENCES: WHY DID THE NORMANS BUILD CASTLES AND CATHEDRALS?

1 Where did the Normans build castles?
2 What kinds of castles did they build?
3 Why did they build so many castles after 1066?
4 What changes did the Normans make to cathedrals?
5 Why did Normans build or alter cathedrals?
6 Look at Seenat's answer at the top of the page. Can you give a better answer now?

Source B

Castles were built after 1066 to keep control over the defeated English. These castles were very important because they helped a small number of Normans (about ten thousand) conquer a far bigger number of English (about two million). This kind of castle was called a motte-and-bailey castle and could be built very quickly. Can you work out why they could be built easily? (See also page 38.)

Castles certainly did help to control England. For example, the people in the south west did not want William as their king. In 1068 he led an army to Exeter and besieged the town. When the local people surrendered William 'selected a spot within the walls for the erection of a castle'. The English must have felt both angry and frightened whenever they looked at the castle. It reminded them how powerful the Normans were and so reduced the chance for another rebellion. If the English did attack, the Normans had a secure fort for protection and for their stores and weapons.

Source C

This map shows the castles that were built in the 20 years after the Norman Conquest. Many were in important towns but many others were on the borders of England and on the coasts. These castles were built to help the Normans keep control. In Wales, the Normans controlled the lowlands and the river valleys with a chain of castles, but the Welsh princes still ruled from the mountain regions and presented a constant threat. So the castles on the Welsh border were needed to prevent both local revolts and attacks from the Welsh princes trying to regain their lands.

The coasts also needed guarding, this time against attacks by Vikings from Scandanavia. The kings of Norway and Denmark both tried to invade England between 1066 and William the Conqueror's death, in 1087.

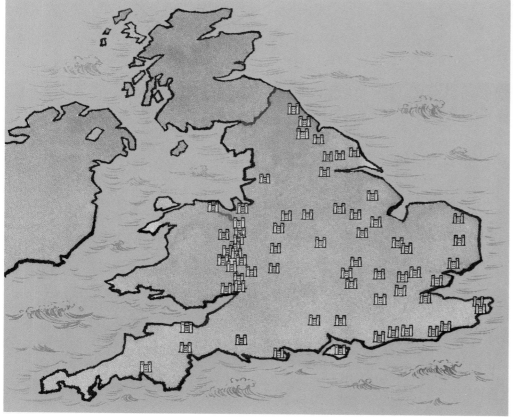

Source D

The Normans also rebuilt a lot of cathedrals, destroying the existing English ones. In some cases the cathedral site was moved from a small village to a big trading centre. For example, the cathedral at North Elmham was resited, firstly at Thetford and then at Norwich. This meant that more people could pray in the cathedral and also that more people were influenced by the bishop. Remember there were no radios or televisions in medieval times and so the king used his bishops to give his 'Party Political Broadcasts'. Many of the English bishops were replaced by Normans by the 1080s.

This map shows how many English cathedrals and large abbeys were rebuilt from 1066 to 1100.

Timeline 1025–1500

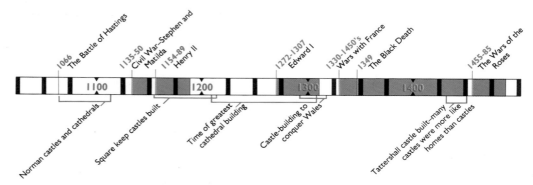

Source E

The Norman cathedrals were much bigger than English ones. They had great, round pillars and wide arches. They looked powerful and impressive, so even the cathedrals reminded the English that the Normans were powerful, that they intended staying in England and that they considered the English were inferior. In short, the Normans were the new rulers.

This picture shows Rochester Cathedral.

⟫⟫ Building castles and cathedrals, 1100–1500

In the years after 1066, the Normans used their castles and cathedrals to show the English that they had new masters. However, building did not stop when the Normans felt safe from rebellion.

People still needed castles and cathedrals throughout the Middle Ages. Use the information on pages 11–14 to answer the questions below.

CAUSES AND CONSEQUENCES: WHY WERE CASTLES AND CATHEDRALS NEEDED?

1 What evidence can you find on pages 11–14 to show that:
  a Warfare was an important part of medieval life?
  b English kings built castles to defend their borders?
  c English kings built castles to help them control new lands?

2 What other reasons were there for building castles?
3 Why did people keep improving their cathedrals throughout the Middle Ages?
4 Between 1200 and 1330 there was a lot of building work at cathedrals. Why was there more building at that time?

⟫⟫ Castles 1100–1500: why were they needed?

In the years after 1066, England was covered by castles which dominated river crossings, roadways and all lines of communication as well as towns. But, gradually, these castles were used for other things besides defence. William had rewarded his followers by giving them land and these great landowners or barons wanted castles in which they could live with their families. So, in addition to their military role, castles became homes for the baron and his family and his soldiers and servants.

Castles also became the local centres of government. The king did not have his own army or police force. Instead he depended on his barons and the sheriffs of each county. The sheriff's job was to arrest criminals and collect taxes and to make sure people kept the laws. Together, the barons and sheriffs were expected to prevent rebellion and guard against invasion. The castles in important towns were used by the sheriffs and barons as their centres of government, rather like town halls and police stations today.

Source F

Here you can see the inside of a twelfth century keep. What clues tell you about the ways the castle was used?

Castles helped the king to govern the country as long as the barons co-operated with the king. But this did not always happen. Between 1135 and 1150 there was a civil war over who should be king. The supporters of Stephen or Matilda strengthened their castles but many other barons built castles as a way of increasing their own power. Later, Henry II had these castles torn down. He said that anyone who wanted to build a castle or add fortifications to their home had to get the king's permission.

Although there were more civil wars later and local barons often had feuds with each other, England gradually became more peaceful. As a result, castles became more and more like homes. The greatest changes happened in the fourteenth and fifteenth centuries. By 1500 castles still looked quite like fortresses from the outside but inside they were becoming very comfortable. Look at Tattershall Castle (Source G). How is it a combination of a fortress and a home?

Castles did not disappear completely in these peaceful areas because the idea of warfare was still important to the barons. Many of the noblemen who built castles had fought in wars against France and it was important to them to show how strong and rich they were. And one of the ways of doing this was by building, or enlarging, a castle.

However, there were more urgent reasons for building new castles in other parts of the country. The reign of Henry II gives us some good examples. Henry was a very powerful king who governed a huge empire, but

Source G

Tattershall Castle in Lincolnshire was built in the fifteenth century. It was made of brick rather than stone.

Source B

This picture of workmen was drawn in the thirteenth century by Matthew Paris, a monk at St. Albans Abbey

Source C

Plans for a medieval building. A master-mason drew this on a plaster board.

Source D

Medieval stonemasons at work

Source E

A stonemason at work at York Minster in the 1980's.

MEDIEVAL TOOLS AND SKILLS

3 Which of the tools and equipment in Sources A and B are still used today?

4 Architect's drawings are usually produced by computer today. How did medieval masons draw their plans?

5 Look at Sources D and E. Do you think that stonemasons today:
  a have an easier job than medieval masons because they have different, high technology tools?
  b do a better job than medieval stonemasons?

6 Does the evidence on these pages support the answer of Seenat or the answer of Joe? Explain the reasons for your choice.

🌊 Who were the builders?

A lot of building tools are just the same today as they were a thousand years ago. That tells us that medieval builders were intelligent and skilful enough to make and use tools that we can't improve. However, they did have disadvantages. Nearly all jobs had to be done by hand, instead of by machines or by computers.

The men who organised this work had to know what they were doing or the castles and cathedrals would never have been finished. These pages help you find out about the people who actually did the building. What does the evidence tell you about their intelligence and skill? Does it support Joe or Seenat?

Source F

A king discussing building work with his master mason. This was drawn by Matthew Paris in the thirteenth century.

The master mason

Source F shows a king talking to a master mason — the man in charge of a building. What skills did the master mason need? How did he organise the men working on the building behind him? Unfortunately, the picture can't answer these questions and nor can the buildings themselves — the castles and cathedrals. Instead we need to look at other sources, such as letters and bills.

Source G

Sirs,

You should know that we have kept on masons, stone cutters, quarrymen and minor workmen all through the winter for making mortar and breaking up stone for lime; we have carts bringing this stone to the site and bringing timber for erecting the buildings in which we are all now living inside the castle; we also have 1000 carpenters, smiths, plasterers and labourers.

If the king wants the work to be finished as quickly as it should be and on the scale we have begun we need at least £250 a week. If we cannot have so much money, let us know.

In case you should wonder where so much money goes we shall need 400 masons and 2000 minor workmen; 100 carts, 60 waggons and 30 boats bringing stone and seacoal; 200 quarrymen; 30 smiths and carpenters.

As for the progress of work, some of the wall stands 28 feet high and even where it is lowest it is 20 feet. We have begun ten of the outer and four of the inner towers. Four gates have been hung and are shut and locked at night.

May God protect your dearest lordships.

(A letter from the master mason at Beaumaris Castle to the King's treasurers, 27 February 1296)

Source H

For a shipload of Caen freestone, £7.
To a woman of Eye for sand, 6s.
For 2 cart loads of charcoal, 3s 2d.
To Mauriçe of Water for timber, £4 13s 4d.
To Richard the cooper for half a dozen buckets, 2s 1d.

(Extracts from a list of payments for work in the construction of Westminister Abbey in 1253)

Source I

Canterbury cathedral was badly damaged by fire in 1174. Then 'mastermasons, both French and English, were assembled; but they disagreed in their opinions; some undertook to repair while others said that the whole church must be taken down.

Among the mastermasons was William of Sens, a man of great abilities, and a most skilful workman in wood and stone. Him they chose for the undertaking'.

(From a chronicle written in the early 1200s by a monk, Gervase of Canterbury)

1   In Source I, Gervase suggests some of the important skills a master mason needed. What were they?
2   The master mason was responsible for all parts of building work. What does Source H tell us about the things he had to organise?

3   What does Source G tell you about the skills and responsibilities of the master mason?
4   Look again at Sources F to I. Do you think that the master mason had to be an intelligent and practical man? Explain the reasons for your answer.

The builders: how were they organised?

In July 1286 the master mason at Harlech castle was in charge of over 900 workmen. The wages bill (Source J) for that month shows that the men were organised into smaller working groups. Each group of craftsmen belonged to a guild which worked from its own lodge building and had its own master. Sources K and L tell us about these guilds.

Source J

The wages bill of men working at Harlech from 2–23 June 1286

Group	Numbers of workers	Wages (£ s d)	Typical daily rate per man
Masons	199	57 10 0	4d–2d
Quarrymen	93	19 13 6	3d–2d
Smiths	18	4 7 6	3d–2d
Carpenters	22	6 14 6	4d–2d
Labourers	572	61 1 0	2d–1d
Clerks	4	1 4 3	4d

Source K

This indenture witnesses that Nicholas, son of John de Kyghlay, shall serve well and faithfully in the manner of an apprentice to John de Bradlay of York from the feast of St Peter to the end of seven years; and Nicholas shall willingly do the orders of his master, keeping the secrets of his master and keeping his counsel. Within this term, John de Bradlay shall instruct and inform Nicholas his apprentice in his craft, and in the buying and selling as belongs to his craft, in the best manner that he knows without concealment; and shall provide food and drink, linen and woollen clothes, bed and footwear.

For which teaching, de Kyghlay shall give to John de Bradlay, six shillings and eight pence for each of the next three years.

(Indenture of an apprentice of York in 1371. An *indenture* was an agreement or contract between two people, saying what each person would do for the other)

Source L

The masons shall be, each morning, at their work in the mason's lodge, as early as they may skilfully see by daylight; and they shall stand there truly working all the day after, as long as they may skilfully see; they may dine at noon if they will; and if any man goes from the lodge and from his work he shall be punished by payment of a fine as agreed by the master. And it is ordered that no mason shall be received to work until he has first proved, a week or more, his good working; and if he is found good at his work and receives the agreement of the master and the mastermason, he shall be hired at work.

(Agreement made between the master of the masons' guild and the Chapter of York Minster in 1370)

1   What different tasks would each group of workmen do?
2   What rules did the guild master have to enforce?

3   How did young men become craftsmen?
4   Do you think that craftsmen had to be skilful to be successful?

🌊 Did they know what they were doing?

If you look at castles today it's often difficult to imagine what they were like in the Middle Ages. Today most have no roofs, no windows, no doors and have half fallen down. But were they always a mess like that? Did William of Sens, or any of the other master masons, just use any old bits of wood or stone and pile them up in any manner, or did they know what they were doing? The next four pages will help you find out how good their technical understanding was. Draw a chart like the one on page 21 and fill in each line when you have looked at the evidence.

What materials did they use?

Stone, wood and clay were the most common building materials. Iron, lead and tin were only available in small quantities. In general, the builders chose wood if they wanted to build quickly and cheaply. They chose stone if they wanted strong, durable constructions. Later in the Middle Ages brick became popular as it was cheaper than stone and easier to cut and move.

Sometimes builders were able to use materials that were lying about nearby. In 1223 stone was taken from the castle ditch at Lincoln to use on the new cathedral building. However, stone was usually brought to the building site from quarries. Source M shows the bill for the stone used to build Westminster Abbey. The different types of stone were:

Caen stone: a strong limestone which cuts well for building blocks.
Marble: a very hard stone which shines when polished.
Chalk: a light stone which can be crushed or cut easily.

HOW DO YOU MAKE SPACE FOR WINDOWS AND DOORS WITHOUT WEAKENING A WALL ?

WHAT ARE DIFFERENT KINDS OF STONE FOR ?

HOW DO YOU MAKE SURE A WALL IS STRONG ENOUGH TO STAND FOR HUNDREDS OF YEARS ?

Source M

For 2 shiploads of Caen stone.   **£12**
To Adam of Aldwych for cutting 55 hundredweight of chalk for the vaults.   **14s 8d.**
For marble at Corfe.   **£18 19s 0d.**

(Building accounts for Westminster Abbey in 1253)

USING DIFFERENT KINDS OF STONE

1 Which stone was good for making wall blocks?
2 Which was good for rubble in foundations?
3 Which was good for stone ceilings (vaults)?
4 Which was good for sculptures and coverings?
5 What did they use to build their temporary workshops and scaffolding?

Now fill in line 1 of your chart

Medieval builders knew the answers to these questions. They chose the type of stone which best suited the job and then chose the quarries that could provide that stone. Transporting heavy stone was a slow and expensive job so stones were always cut to shape at the quarry to avoid moving waste material. Planning how to get the stone cheaply to the site was another skill.

Did they understand about	YES	Sometimes	NO	Not sure
the uses of different kinds of stone?				
... building a strong wall by				
using pointed arches?				
using strong foundations?				
using good stone-laying techniques?				
using buttresses for support?				

Use this chart to record your answers as you work through this section.

Did they know how to build strong walls?

Castles and cathedrals both needed strong walls. Castle walls had to be strong to stop attacks by missiles or battering rams. Cathedral walls had to be strong because they were so tall and supported heavy towers, spires, ceilings and roofs.

If you want to build a strong wall you need to make sure that:

- the wall doesn't fall over while you're building it,
- the wall doesn't fall over after you've finished,
- the wall doesn't sink down into the ground,
- the wall doesn't crack

Did the medieval builders know these rules? Pages 21–24 help you answer this question.

Foundations

Large buildings need good foundations, Without them, walls will fall over during or after building, they may crack or sink into the ground. Read the clues about medieval foundations *then fill in line 3 of your chart.*

Clue A
Repair work at York Minster allows you to see the foundations. The size of the foundations and the pillar make the modern radiator look very small.

Clue B
It was noted in 1320 that the new work at Hereford Cathedral was to be built on 'the ancient foundation which is thought to be firm and solid in the judgement of masons regarded as skilled in their art'.

Clue C
At Farnham Castle foundations were 7.3 metres deep and 11.9 metres square.

Clue D
The foundations for the central tower at Wells Cathedral sank 15 years after the scaffolding was removed and major repair work was needed.

Clue E
The great tower of Winchester Cathedral fell down in 1107. Some people thought this happened because William Rufus (an unreligious king) had been buried there but William of Malmesbury a 12th century historian, wrote that 'it was due to bad foundations'.

Stonework

A strong wall must be built carefully. It must go straight up, with vertical faces, and the lines of stonework must be horizontal. The stone blocks must also be held together in a strong wall.

Medieval builders used a lime mortar between the stone blocks of a wall. This prevented the blocks grinding together on top of each other, which often caused splitting. The mortar also gripped the stone and so made the wall stronger.

Mortar was made by mixing lime (made from burning crushed limestone) with sand and water. This mixture slowly hardened as

Making walls strong

Medieval walls were also designed like a sandwich. Each stone wall had regular blocks on the outside and inside faces but there was rubble in between. This sandwich effect made the walls cheaper to build. It also meant that the faces could move independently if the foundations were weak. As a result, the sandwich walls were less likely to crack than the solid ones. Walls were also thicker at the bottom than at the top and this made them very stable.

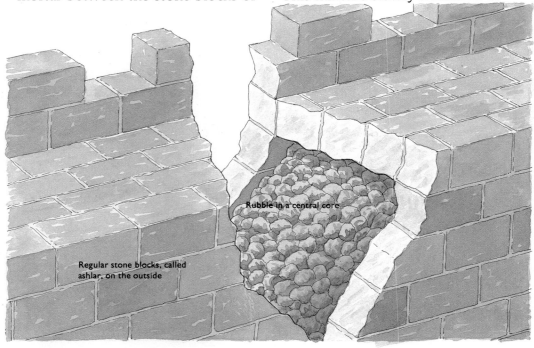

Regular stone blocks, called ashlar, on the outside

Rubble in a central core

Flying buttress. The weighted pinnacle makes the buttress firm

Buttresses

The builders used a third method to ensure that cathedral walls were strong. They used buttresses to prop the walls up. The Norman buttress is not very effective. Although it is broad, it is not deep enough. It is very difficult to prop something up if you are so close to it. The thirteenth century buttress is better. The flying buttress is best of all. It starts away from the base of the wall and then leans in at the top. It also has a heavy weight pressing down which makes the buttress firm.

Thirteenth century buttress

Norman buttress

the water evaporated and the lime combined with carbon dioxide in the air.

But that's all a twentieth century explanation; did the medieval builders know this about lime mortar? Well, the answer is probably that they didn't. What they did know was that the wet mortar cracked easily in the winter frosts so they didn't build in the winter. Instead they covered the tops of the partly finished walls with straw. And they knew that walls and towers often fell if they were built too quickly, without leaving enough time for the mortar to harden.

Arches

The arches in Norman cathedrals were semi-circular. The top of doorways and windows in Norman castles and cathedrals also had this circular arch shape. Later arches were pointed. The geometry of the two arch types is different. A pointed arch can be made with any height and width. A round arch can only be made higher if it is also made wider. What are the advantages of using a pointed arch?
A wooden frame, called centring, was used to support an arch while it was being built. It was needed until the top stone, the key stone, was put into place. This key stone locked all the stones into place. The centring was then taken down.

Norman arched doorway

13th century arched doorway

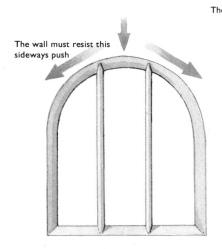

The arrows show the way the loads are carried to the ground

The wall must resist this sideways push

Norman semicircular arch

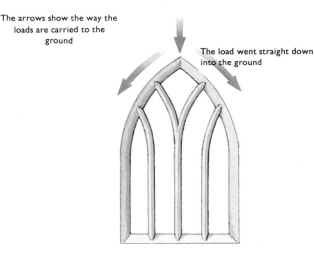

The load went straight down into the ground

Pointed arch

Do windows weaken walls?

Strong walls are very useful but they need windows and doors to let people in, to let light in and for shooting arrows. These holes could make the wall weaker so the Normans made sure their windows were always small and far apart. Later windows became bigger and closer together without weakening the walls. Nowadays, we know that this change was safe because the later builders used pointed arches instead of round ones. Do you think the medieval builders understood why this worked? The weight of the wall and roof above a hole is called the load. This load is passed both downwards and outwards by the round arch. So the wall alongside the window must be strong enough to support this outward force. If there were too many windows close together, the wall was weak.
A pointed arch passes the load straight down. The wall doesn't need to give extra support for the load. So you can have more windows close together without weakening the wall.

COULD THEY BUILD STRONG WALLS?

Look at Source B on page 17
1 Are the lines of stone horizontal? What tool did the builders use to help them?
2 Are the faces of the wall vertical? What tool helped the builders?
3 What can we learn about the practical skills and powers of observation of

medieval builders from:
a mortar
b buttresses
c arches
d windows

Now fill in lines 2, 4 and 5 of your chart

Stone vaults

The Normans built some cathedrals with stone ceilings, called vaults. These were round-arch barrel vaults. But the load pattern of the round arches meant that the weight of the ceiling and the roof pushed the walls outwards. So vaults could not be big or heavy. Later vaults had pointed arches.

Their loads went down through the walls. This allowed the builders to make the vaults bigger and heavier. The geometry of the pointed arch also allowed them to vary the width and the height of the vaults.

We do not know why vaults were so popular in cathedrals. Perhaps it was because they were fire resistant or because they looked more impressive than the wooden roofing beams above them.

Looking up at a stone vaulted ceiling from the nave of a cathedral

So did they *really* know what they were doing?

Today, civil engineers and architects who design large buildings learn about the 'Theory of Structures' — all about the building loads and the wind loads and their effect on the walls and foundations. They can easily describe the effects of pointed arches, foundations and buttresses.

However, it's difficult to know how much a medieval builder understood. No one wrote down their ideas at the time so we only have the evidence from the buildings themselves. The example of the foundations for the two cathedrals suggests they had some understanding but that it wasn't perfect.

How did they learn that the pointed windows could be put close together? We don't know that either. Sometimes they must have learned by trial and error. There are a lot of written records telling of walls and towers collapsing. But it was expensive and dangerous if they only learnt from their mistakes. Sometimes they must have learnt by studying other things — a buttress is like a prop for a haystack and a pointed arch is the same as the shape made by a loop of heavy chain hanging down. But we don't know for sure.

All we can do is look at the results and think about what the medieval builders achieved. When Ely Cathedral was built, for example, the tracks and bridges leading to the site were strengthened before the stone was delivered. And corner posts, over 20 metres long and weighing 10 tonnes, were lifted up 30 metres to build the Octagonal Tower.

So do you think they knew what they were doing? The answers in your chart should help you answer this.

✼ Conclusions: were medieval builders skilful?

What have you learned in this chapter about the skills and intelligence of medieval people? Look back at Seenat and Joe's answers on page 16. Which of them do you agree with now? Or can you think of a better answer of your own? It may help you to think about the ideas in the spider diagram on the right.

Understanding how to use different materials

The organization of hundreds of workmen

Understanding different ways of strengthening walls

Simple tools and equipment

Were medieval builders skilful?

The training given to craftsmen

The skills of the master-mason

Understanding the use of arches and vaults

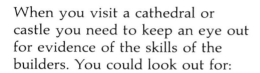 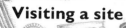 **Visiting a site**

When you visit a cathedral or castle you need to keep an eye out for evidence of the skills of the builders. You could look out for:

● different kinds of stonework and where they are used.
● different window shapes. The higher pointed arches should be in which parts of the building – the older or the newer?
● buttresses – are there different kinds?
● modern building work – are the workmen using any tools which the medieval builders used?

This is also a good chance to use your imagination. Stand back and look upwards. How did they get stone up there, so high? What was it like to be responsible for the building as a master mason? How would you have felt when a great archway, or window or tower was completed? Would you have been a good master mason?

If a craftsman came to your building site and asked for work what questions would you have asked him about his skills and methods?

Using the sources as evidence

In this chapter you have been using a variety of sources which tell us about the building of castles and cathedrals. Historians cannot work without sources so they need to know what kinds of sources are available and how useful they are. Can you answer these questions?

USING THE SOURCES AS EVIDENCE

1 In this chapter you used three kinds of primary sources from the Middle Ages.
 a One kind of source was the written records. List three different examples of written records from this chapter.
 b A second kind of source was the medieval illustrations. Give three examples of medieval illustrations.
 c What is the other main source of evidence for how castles and cathedrals were built?
2 Which kind of source would be most useful if you were investigating:
 a medieval tools and equipment,

 b the people who did the building,
 c how much the builders knew about the technology of building?
3 In this chapter you read different kinds of written sources. Explain why you think each of these examples would or would not be reliable evidence.
 a The wages list for Harlech Castle in 1286 (Source J, page 19).
 b The letter from the master mason at Beaumaris Castle in 1296 (Source G, page 18).
 c The agreement made at York Minster in 1370 (Source L, page 19).

Was life comfortable in castles and cathedrals?

NO, THEY DIDN'T HAVE ELECTRIC LIGHTS OR CENTRAL HEATING...

...AND NO TELEVISION OR VIDEO, EVEN IF THEY WERE RICH.

In the last chapter you investigated the people who built the castles and cathedrals. This chapter will also investigate people — the people who lived and worked in them after they were built.

It is easy to forget about these people because we only notice the buildings and the tourists when we visit a castle or cathedral today; and the stone looks cold, grey and uncomfortable as if no-one had ever really lived there. But it *is* possible to find evidence about the people of the Middle Ages. For example, archaeologists excavating Sandal castle found sewing thimbles. Flutes were found at White Castle. Are you surprised?

When you imagine a medieval scene in a castle or cathedral it is often dark and gloomy. In films, like Robin Hood, everyone seems to be dressed in muddy brown or green. There are no bright colours anywhere. And if you look at some stone carvings, especially ones outside buildings which have been damaged by the weather, it looks as if medieval people were clumsy and made models like young children.

Look at the evidence on pages 26–29. Use it to answer the question 'Was life comfortable in castles and cathedrals?' Was life more comfortable, colourful and artistic than you first thought?

Source A

This room has been redecorated to show what a room in a medieval castle was like. This is the Queen's daybed in Leeds Castle, Kent.

In 1267 the building accounts for the king's buildings at Westminster record:
For gold leaf and other things necessary for paintings around the king's bed in the king's chamber, £53 5s 2d.

There were other comforts too. Baths were common and accounts give details of the payments made for having the water heated and carried to the king's chamber.

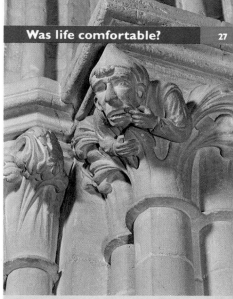

Source B
Medieval stonemasons added lifelike carvings to churches and cathedrals. Sometimes the faces were those of other workmen. This poor man at Wells cathedral has toothache.

Source C
Large and detailed stone carvings like this were made for many cathedrals and large churches. You can see this one if you visit Winchester Cathedral.

Source D
Many parish churches were covered with wall paintings like this one from Kempley in Gloucestershire.

Source E
People's clothes helped to make medieval buildings colourful. This scene shows the wedding of the Duchess of Berry. The rich also had colourful illustrations like this in their prayer books.

Source F
These effigies (full size carvings on graves) are of Henry IV and his wife Joanna of Navarre. They were buried in Canterbury Cathedral. You can see effigies in many parish churches where the local lord was buried.

Source G
This stained glass window is from Canterbury Cathedral. Stained glass became more common later in the Middle Ages.

Source H

Buildings were full of delicate little carvings like this scene from Lincoln Cathedral.

Source I

Floors were also decorated. These tiles are from Cleeve Abbey in Somerset.

Source J

Metalwork was just as delicate as woodwork. This candlestick was made for Gloucester Cathedral. Can you imagine how many hours it took to make and what it would cost to make today?

Visiting a site

When you visit a castle or cathedral it is often difficult to see things because the building is so huge. This isn't as daft as it sounds! Most people gaze around and crane their necks upwards to look at the ceiling or battlements. It's hard to stop doing that and look closely at the details of the building. If you do hunt for details you can find plenty of clues about what life was like in castles and cathedrals. Here are some clues to look for.

Were people interested in comfort and beauty in the Middle Ages?

Castles

Look out for:

- the size of windows and doors
- carvings in wood and stone
- kitchens and fireplaces
- chapels
- what the lord's rooms looked like

Cathedrals

Look out for:

- windows and glass
- carvings in wood and stone
- colours on paintings, effigies and windows
- what the buildings in a monastery were used for

Don't forget to investigate the local museum for more evidence found at the site

Daily life in the cathedrals

Source K

12 midnight	Service of Matins
1 am	Service of Lauds
6 am	Service of Prime
8 am	Service of Tierce
10 am	High Mass
12 noon	Service of Sext
3 pm	Service of None
6 pm	Service of Vespers
8 pm	Service of Evening Prayer

Source L

A plan of Worcester Cathedral. The dotted lines show where walls would have been.

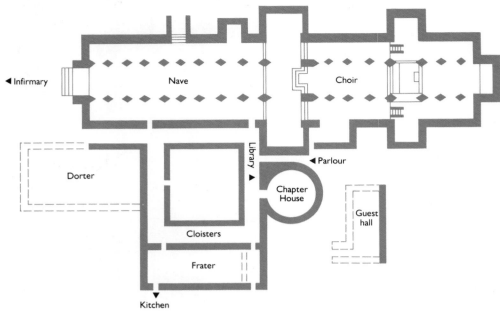

The evidence on pages 26–29 may have surprised you. Medieval people were interested in colour, art and comfort — even castles were colourful places. Cathedrals were also surprising because they were not just used for church services.

Many cathedrals were part of monasteries so the services were led by the abbot (the leader of the monastery) and the monks. Daily life at Worcester Cathedral gives us a good example of life in a monastic cathedral. The monks followed the strict rule of St. Benedict. They promised to give up everything they owned, to stay unmarried and to obey the abbot. They spent their lives in prayer.

Source M

Idleness is the enemy of the soul. Therefore the brethren should be busy at certain times working with their hands and at other times reading godly books.

(Extract from the *Rule of St Benedict*)

Source N

Three fingers write, but the whole body is working. They do not know how to write, who say that it is no labour.

(Extract from *Reliquiae Antiquae*. Reading, writing and schooling took place in the cloisters and the library)

Source O

In the days when the most terrible famine of the year 1197 was raging our monastery gave help to many. Our Abbot, on every flesh eating day, had a whole ox boiled. He gave it out with a piece of bread to every one of the poor. By God's grace all the poor who came to us were kept alive until harvest time.

(From a medieval chronicle. The poor were looked after by the almoner and the hospitaler)

A DAY IN THE LIFE OF A CATHEDRAL

1   Look at the list of services they went to in the cathedral (Source K).
   a   How many services were there?
   b   What was the longest number of hours between services?
   c   What was the shortest number of hours between services?

2   Look at the plan of Worcester Cathedral (Source L). What work did the monks do during the day besides praying? (Use the different parts of the monastery as clues).

3   What can you find out from sources M, N and O about monks' duties?

In addition to praying, the monks spent time eating (in the frater), chatting (in the parlour) and sleeping (in the dorter) just like us today. They attended meetings in the chapter house (to plan their work for the day) and if they were ill or very old they went to the infirmary. They cooked meals (in the kitchen) and collected and stocked food. So in fact a monastery was a busy place with both the monks and the lay brothers — men who had taken only some of the religious vows — doing very ordinary chores.

Daily life in the secular cathedrals

The secular cathedrals were cathedrals without a monastery attached. They were also busy places. The Church was central to the lives of the people. People went there almost every day for services, to meet their neighbours, for news and to have lessons. The poor and the sick also received shelter, food and clothing from the Church.

It's difficult to imagine all these other activities in a cathedral but a typical scene is described by Cynthia Harnett in her book called 'The Load of Unicorn'. The story is about a boy called Bendy who lived in the fifteenth century. In this scene he is going to meet his father in St. Paul's Cathedral — the Norman cathedral which was later burnt down in The Great Fire of 1666.

'As usual it was full of people: country folks with bundles and babies sitting on the floor to rest before starting their tramp home; and Londoners meeting each other to walk up and down and talk business, or engaging servants who waited by a certain pillar to be hired, or consulting lawyers by another pillar, or, as Bendy himself did every day, just using it as a short cut. There was a steady hum of voices all round him, but he noticed how the sound was carried up and lost in the high vaulted roof. At the bottom of the nave stood a row of tables where the scribes sat. Bendy caught a glimpse of his father's silvery head beneath a signboard which read JOHN GOODRICH, SCRIVENER. His father was copying a letter for an old woman in a widow's wimple who sat on a stool beside him.'

Only boys went to school in monasteries. Girls were usually taught at home, or in convents. The monks were often very strict teachers, beating the boys if they forgot what they had been taught.

Source P

Steward (the most important official – in charge)
Wardrober (in charge of the Treasury and the robes)

Clerk of Offices	Larderers
Almoner	Poulterers
Friar	Ushers
Chief buyer	Chandlers
Marshal	Porter
Pantryman	Baker
Butler	Brewer
Boy helpers	Farrier

Daily life in the castles

As you have discovered, castles were not just places for soldiers to attack or defend. They were the homes of wealthy families and of the many people who worked for the lord and his lady. Here is some more evidence about life in castles to help you with your investigation.

THE PEOPLE IN THE CASTLE

1   What sort of jobs do you think the following people did? Marshal, butler, farrier, almoner, ushers, chandlers, friar.
2   Can you think of any jobs which are missing from Source P that would have been needed in a castle?

What did they eat?

We know what people ate in the Middle Ages from household accounts and from recipes. Archaeologists have also discovered fish, bird and animal remains during excavations among kitchen rubbish.

These sources give the impression that medieval people were always tucking into feasts but it would have depended on money (no money, no food) and whether you were the stable boy or the Lord or Lady of the Manor.

Source Q

Grain, 7 bushels		
Wine, 2 sesters 1 gallon		
Ale, by purchase, 188 gallons	**7s 3d**	
Ale, by carriage	**3d**	
Kitchen (fresh meat)		
1 and a half oxen		
3 sheep	**16s**	

FOOD AND DRINK

5   Did medieval people have a vegetarian diet?
6   What foods are missing that we think are important today?

Who lived in the castles?

Lists of prices and wages are very useful sources of evidence about medieval building skills. They also help us to answer the question 'who lived there'? Source P gives a list of some of the officials working for the Baron of Eresby in the thirteenth century.

3   Do you think that all these people were needed in an early Norman castle? Explain your answer.
4   The list doesn't seem to include women.
    a   Why not?
    b   What jobs would they have done?

Calves	**3s 3d**
Hens	**3s 8d**
Kitchen	
200 herring from stores	
Fish bought	**8s 6d**
Butter	**6d**
150 eggs from rents	
Eggs bought	**8d**
Milk for the week, 9 gallons	
2 lbs cinnamon for making sauce	
Stable	
Hay for 31 horses	
Oats, 2 quarters	
Grain, 3 quarters for 46 dogs	
Other	
Grain for the poor and ale	
for the household 3 lbs wax	

(Household accounts for Eleanor, Countess of Leicester for April 1265)

Other accounts show that the Countess bought salt by the bushel (about 36 litres) as well as pepper, ginger, and cloves in smaller quantities of between 1 kg and 4 kg.

7   What do you think the wax was used for?
8   Why was so much salt used?
9   What were the spices for?

What did they wear?

There are many surviving medieval illustrations that show what people wore. Look at the pictures on this page and compare the clothing with the pictures on pages 16 and 17.

Source R

Fine silk from Italy	£4 0s 0d a piece
Fur for trims	
Linen – canvas	2d for an ell
Wool – fine scarlet	7s 0d for an ell
Wool – perse	1s 8d for an ell

(From extracts in various household accounts in the thirteenth century. An ell was about 1.15 metres. Household accounts tell us the types and cost of the materials used in the Middle Ages as well as about the food shown in Source Q)

These pictures show the very colourful and expensive clothes that rich people wore.

Other activities

You have already read about archaeological finds that show that sewing and music were medieval activities but how else did people spend their time?

Source S

To the huntsman and his groom	2s 3d
For the purchase of 2 gerfalcons	£7 6s 8d
To James the Joiner for chessboards (and other items)	66s 6d
For minstrels and musicians	1s–3s each
For acrobats, jugglers, jester and story-tellers	1d–2s each
For a small cart as a plaything	7d

(From extracts in various household accounts in the thirteenth century)

A COMFORTABLE LIFE?

10 How would you describe the clothes in the pictures on this page?

11 Who would have been able to afford to use the different materials in Source R?

12 Do you think that people were always well-dressed in the Middle Ages? You will find evidence in the other pictures in this book.

13 Read Source S. Which activities would:
  a the nobles and their families have taken part in or watched?
  b the servants have taken part in or watched?

14 What do you think was uncomfortable about life in a castle?

Did castles and cathedrals change during the Middle Ages?

? DID THEY ?

? ?

DIDN'T THEY ?

? ?

So far you have investigated why castles and cathedrals were needed and how they were built. You have also studied the people who built and lived in them. These topics should have given you some ideas about how to answer the question above. This chapter will give you some more evidence – about what the buildings looked like. Is it possible to describe one cathedral and say that all others are like it? Were all castles the same? Look at

the evidence on these pages and fill in the grid (below). Then you can answer questions 5–8 and decide whether there was much change in castles and cathedrals during the Middle Ages.

Sources A–D show the floor plans for the two castles and the two cathedrals shown on pages 6 and 7. Firstly, look at the cathedral plans and answer questions 1–3. Put the answers on the grid.

	Are the buildings both the same size? List any differences	Are the buildings both the same shape? List any differences	Do the buildings have the same areas? List any differences
CATHEDRALS Durham – Source A Winchester – Source B			
CASTLES Restormel – Source C Caernarfon – Source D			

CHANGES: HOW DID THE BUILDINGS CHANGE?

1 Are the cathedrals about the same size?
2 Are they about the same shape?
3 Can you find the same areas on both plans?
4 Now look at the two castle plans and answer the same three questions.
5 Look at the answer grid. Describe:
   a the changes in cathedrals

b the continuities in cathedrals
6 Did cathedrals change much in the Middle Ages?
7 Describe:
   a the changes in castles
   b the continuities in castles
8 Did castles change much in the Middle Ages?

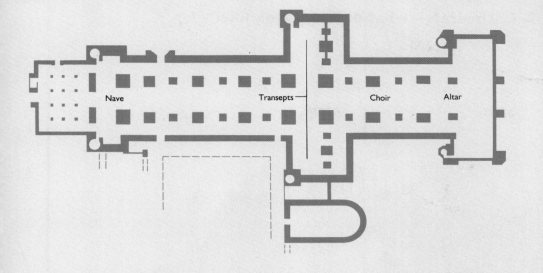

Source A

A ground plan of Durham Cathedral

Nave

Transepts

Choir

Altar

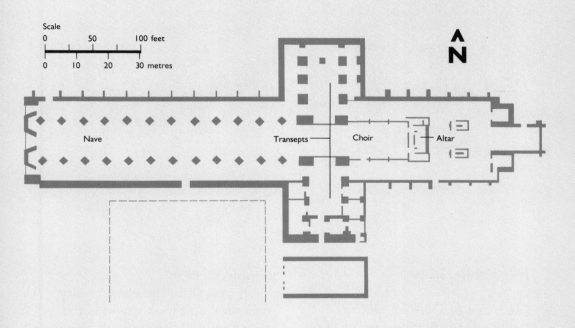

Scale

0   50   100 feet

0   10   20   30 metres

N

Nave

Transepts

Choir

Altar

Source B

A ground plan of Winchester Cathedral

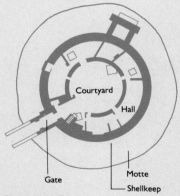

Courtyard

Hall

Gate

Motte

Shellkeep

Source C

A ground plan of Restormel Castle

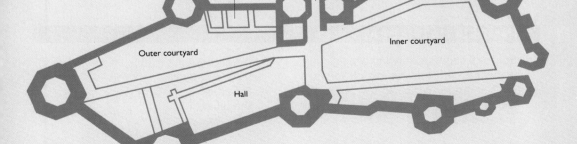

Towers

Kitchens

Gatehouse

Outer courtyard

Inner courtyard

Hall

Source D

A ground plan of Caernarfon Castle

Cathedrals – what did they look like?

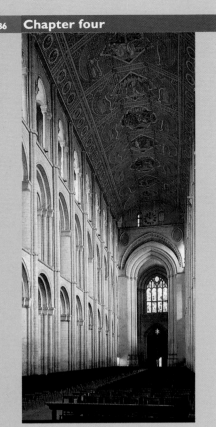

Source E

The nave of Ely Cathedral. This cathedral has a painted wooden ceiling but many cathedrals had stone, vaulted ceilings.

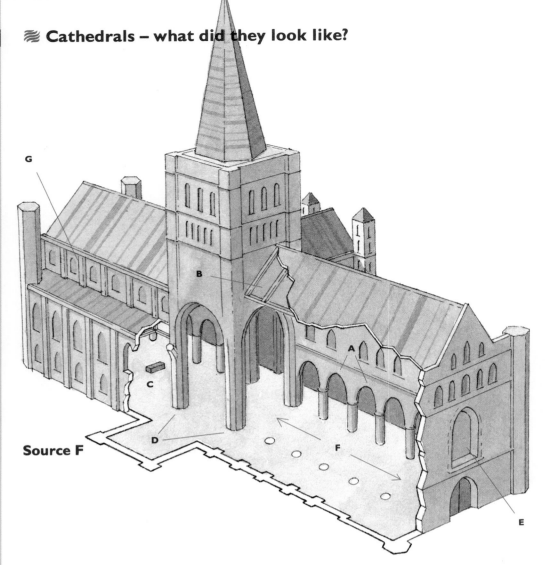

Source F

The similarities

The plans of Durham and Winchester cathedrals are very similar, even though much of Winchester was built 300 years after Durham. The cathedrals are the same shape – cross shaped and pointing in the same direction. The main areas are in the same place; the altar, the aisles, the nave for the people to sit in.

If you sit in the nave of any cathedral and look towards the altar you will see some of the same features. On each side of you is a row of arches with massive pillars. Beyond them is an aisle and the side wall and, looking up, there is a row of clerestory windows on each side, letting in the light. Look at Source E.

INSIDE A CATHEDRAL

I   Source F shows a drawing of a cathedral with the side cut off so you can see inside. Which arrow points to:
the vault?
the aisle?
the arches?
the clerestory?
the altar?
the pillars?
the west window?

The differences

Although the cathedral shape remained unchanged, Chapter 2 showed you that medieval builders made a lot of changes to the shape of arches and windows and to buttresses. So if you look at different cathedrals you'll see differences in the style or design.

Many of the changes in style made the cathedrals look lighter and taller — more beautiful. Today we give names to these different styles.

Look at the photographs on pages 6 and 7. Copy the grid below and fill in the boxes using one word only to describe the features in the left hand column.

	Durham	Winchester
The shape of the arches		
The shape of the windows		
The complexity of the vaults		
The design of the pillars		
Style name	Norman	Gothic
Date	early 12th century	14th century

Why did they change?

Mostly, cathedrals did not *have* to be changed — after all Durham Cathedral was built in the Norman style over 800 years ago and it is still standing. But we know from Chapter 2 that some changes were common sense — the later buttresses were more effective than the Norman ones. And occasionally changes were needed urgently. The builders at Wells Cathedral did have to make changes in 1338 because the tower cracked and it was going to fall down.

This was not the only change they made at Wells as you can see from the following list.

Building began	**1186**
Main building finished	**1239**
New chapel added	**1310**
Choir extended	**1325**
Tower added	**1386**
Another tower added	**1424**

So why were all these changes made?

There are two possible reasons why changes were made in the general style of cathedral building or at any particular cathedral. The builders and designers could have changed things because they *had* to or because they *wanted* to.

Copy out the sentences 1–3 below, adding either 'change was needed' or 'change was wanted' and then answer question 4.

*Do you understand the difference between **had** and **wanted**?*
Joe decided to go swimming but then changed his mind.
Perhaps the lifeguard told him the sea was dangerous, so he **had** to change his mind. This change was needed.
Perhaps he suddenly decided to go shopping instead, so he **wanted** to change his plans. This change was wanted.

REASONS FOR CHANGE

1 Supports were added to hold up the tower at Wells because . . .
2 A new chapel was added at Wells because . . .
3 The Norman cathedral at Winchester was re-built in the new Gothic style because . . .

4 Do you think that medieval people changed the cathedral designs because they had to or because they wanted to?

Castles – what did they look like?

The castles at Restormel and Caernarfon were very different. There had been major changes in castle design between 1100 and 1300. They were not the same shape or size and many of the features had changed. So it is impossible to describe one castle and say that all other castles were the same. The changes were so great that it is clear they were not just changes in fashion. Instead castles changed because their purpose changed. Sometimes wars made defence important, at other times peace meant that castles became more like homes.

These pages show three different types of castle. Look at the pictures and captions carefully before answering the questions below.

Motte and bailey design

● After William won the Battle of Hastings he needed to keep control over the English. The earliest castles had just a motte with a watchtower. (See page 9.)

● The motte was an earth mound, surrounded by a ditch. The owner's hall might be on the motte or in the bailey.

● The bailey was a courtyard with a fence around, usually containing living quarters, stables, workshops and kitchens.

● About 750 of these castles were built in England and Wales.

● In nearly 70%, the motte was less than 5m high.

THE DEVELOPMENT OF CASTLES

1 When was each castle built?
2 What materials was each castle made from?
3 Which castle could be built most quickly? Explain the reasons for your answer.
4 Would each castle frighten away attackers?
5 What were the weaknesses of each castle if it was attacked?
6 Which castle was most comfortable to live in?
7 Explain how wars and peace helped to change castles.

Edwardian design

Edward I conquered Wales even though the Welsh fought hard to keep their independence. Edward then built a ring of strong castles around Wales. He intended to bring Wales under permanent English control.

- Castle building in Wales continued for over 50 years.
- Today these castles would cost tens of millions of pounds.
- The designs included all the latest ideas seen by the soldiers fighting on the Crusades in the Middle East. For example, the inside walls were higher than the outside walls. Defenders on the inside walls could then fire over the heads of the defenders on the outside walls. This was known as the concentric design.
- Stone was transported by sea to some of the sites.
- Comfortable living quarters were provided for the king and the castle commanders.

This is a picture of Conwy castle

Residential castles and fortified manor houses

Kirby Muxloe castle was built for Lord Hastings, Chamberlain of the Royal Household and Edward IV's closest friend. He was one of the wealthiest nobles in the fifteenth century.

- Building began in 1480 but was left unfinished when Lord Hastings was executed in 1483 by Richard III.
- The castle was made of brick and stone. The bricks were made near the castle and were a sign that the owner wanted the latest fashion in building.
- The castle had a kitchen, a pantry, dovecots, fireplaces, garderobes (toilets) and a Great Hall with a Solar at one end – a separate, sunny room for the owner and his wife.
- The family badge and Lord Hastings' initials are made in brick patterns on the gatehouse turrets, beside the gun ports.

Which castle design was best?

These three castle designs are all very different. But there is no 'Best Castle Award'. Each design fits well with its use. When the use changed so the design changed. But don't be misled by the dates – not all the castle styles were the same at any one time. Kirby Muxloe was built firstly for comfort and only secondly for defence but remember that the needs were different on the south coast and up in the borders. For example, the King of Scotland was still building Stirling Castle for defence against the English nearly 20 years after Kirby Muxloe was built for comfort.

≋ Why did castles change?

Castles changed for several reasons. Kings built them to control the people and defend the country. Later castles became larger and more comfortable. Castles also changed because weapons and methods of warfare changed.

At the beginning of the Middle Ages a castle could be attacked by men with crossbows, swords, long bows and pikes. But by the end of the period small cannons, catapults with rocks and other methods were used. Each time the attackers thought up a new idea the castle builders had to think up a new way to protect the defenders.

The motte and bailey castles were quick to build (the motte at York only took seven days) and were good at reminding the English people that they had been beaten. But they were very weak against a determined attacker. The wooden walls could be burnt or chopped down or just climbed over with ladders.

There were many ways of attacking a castle. This picture shows you some of them.
You could make a wall collapse by tunnelling under it or you could use different kinds of machines to hurl missiles. A ballista was a huge crossbow. Trebuchets and mangonels were like catapults, throwing massive boulders.

When a castle was first attacked
the defenders sent down showers
of arrows. This arrow storm could
be so fierce that the attackers had
to shelter behind man-size
wooden shields.

If the attackers reached the castle
walls the defenders could trap
them in the gatehouse, by
dropping the portcullis behind
them. Then the defenders could
pour boiling water and drop
stones through the murder holes
in the roof and fire arrows
through the loop holes at the sides.

So castle design *had* to change.
Some of the early wooden motte
and bailey designs were rebuilt in
stone, to the same design. They
had walkways round the inside of
the wall to give the defender an
advantage. However, the earth
mottes were not usually strong
enough to support a heavy stone
building. So the Normans started
to design stone 'keeps' as well.
These were strong square towers,
like the White Tower at the Tower
of London, built on solid ground
with massive walls over five metres
thick and up to forty metres high.

This change seemed to make
things impossible for an attacker.
The tower was too high to climb
into at the top and anyway the
defenders would be up there, firing
arrows from behind the
battlements. The main door was up
on the first floor level with only a
steep wooden stairway to it; so

they couldn't batter the door down
easily.

At first the only way to capture
these keeps was to lay siege, to sit
outside and wait until the defenders
ran out of food, water and arrows.
But soon attackers thought up new
ideas. The square corners of the
keep were weak. They collapsed if
attackers built tunnels underneath
and dug away at the foundations.
And then they began to design
machines to throw boulders and
batter the walls.

The design of the castles *had* to
change again and changes came
thick and fast, particularly when the
soldiers returning from the
Crusades talked about the castles
they had seen abroad. To the right
you can see a list of changes in
castle building. Can you match the
right reason to each change to
explain why they happened?

Changes

1   Outer (curtain) walls added.
2   Towers added to the wall.
3   Towers made round.
4   Water filled moats added.
5   Gatehouse added with
    portcullis and drawbridge.

Reasons

a   Avoided the weakness of
    corners.
b   Prevented attackers reaching
    the keep.
c   Prevented attackers charging
    through the main entrance.
d   Prevented attackers sneaking
    along the wall. Eliminated
    blind spots.
e   Prevented mining.

Source G

To Richard Leyne and his 5 mates for carrying 6 cartloads from Haslebury to the castle.   **12s. 0d.**

To Godwin de Ymtrema for a bucket.   **2d.**

(From the accounts for Winchester Castle for 9 July 1222)

〽 Why else did castles and cathedrals change?

We've missed something out. When we looked at the reasons why castles and cathedrals were built and why they had changed we forgot one important factor — money! Without money nothing was built and nothing was changed. Every craftsman or trader had to be paid — even if they only supplied a bucket (Source G). However, as Source H shows, sometimes the costs and the problems were much greater.

Source H

Sirs,

You should know that when this letter was written we were short of £500. The men's pay has been and still is very much in arrears, and we are having the greatest difficulty in keeping them because they simply have nothing to live on.

May God protect your dearest lordships.

P.S. And sirs be quick with the money for the works; otherwise everything done up till now will have been of no avail.

(Letter from the mastermason at Beaumaris Castle to the King's treasurers, 1296)

〽 Where did the money come from?

In the Middle Ages the king, the church and the barons were all land owners. For example, at the time of the Domesday Survey, two thirds of all the land in Worcestershire was owned by the church. And so the land provided a source of money from rents and the sale of surplus crops. This paid for much of the building because, for most of the Middle Ages, landowners made good profits from their land. However, there were other ways of paying for building work.

Source I

The king greets Engelard, Constable of Windsor. We order you not to hinder over tolls those who come to the wood for timber for the work of our castle of Winchester but to let them have free passage through the forest, helping them in the carriage.

(Writ for works at Winchester Castle in 1222)

Source J

The king greets Richard de Munfichet. We order you that you should let the Constable of Dover have for the work of our castle as many tree-trunks as are sufficient to make 100 joists, in such a way that all the timber that can be made from those trunks shall be used for our purposes and for our profit.

(Writ for works at Dover castle in 1222)

Source K

In 1181 appeals were made for more money for Ripon Cathedral. Subscribers were promised that 'as long as they lived a mass would be sung for them every day and when they died another mass would be celebrated for their souls and for the souls of all their ancestors in relief of the penalties of their sins.'

(Extract from an appeal by Ripon Chapter, 1181)

PAYING FOR THE BUILDINGS

1   What do Sources I and J tell us about the way the king got materials for his buildings?

2   What does Source K tell us about the way money was raised to build Ripon Cathedral?

Conclusions: did castles and cathedrals change in the Middle Ages?

	Evidence for change	Evidence for continuity
CASTLES	Designs changed – castles were different shapes and sizes	Castles were always used for defence on the borders
	Castles changed because of improved weapons	Castles were always a mixture of home and fortress
	Some castles became more like homes than fortresses	Nobles governed their areas from their castles
CATHEDRALS	Many cathedrals were rebuilt and became larger	Cathedrals stayed the same shape
	New styles of building developed, e.g. pointed arches	Cathedrals had the same parts, e.g. nave, transepts, etc.
	Changes were needed if walls or towers were weak	Cathedrals were always an important part of everyday life because religion stayed important

CHANGES: DID CASTLES AND CATHEDRALS CHANGE?

1 Look at the grid above. What evidence could you use to support each of Joe and Seenat's answers?

2 Which answer do you agree with or do you have one of your own?

Historians often disagree about the past, just like Joe and Seenat. Two historians might disagree because:

● they visited different castles and cathedrals to look for evidence.

● one just studied the Middle Ages but the other historian compared the Middle Ages with change in the twentieth century.

DIFFERENT VIEWS: WAS THERE CHANGE IN THE MIDDLE AGES?

3 Why would these two reasons make historians disagree?

4 If two historians disagree does that mean that one of them is right and the other is wrong?

Visiting a site

When you visit a site you need to think about whether it was all built at once or whether it was built in stages over a long time. Many castles and cathedrals were added to, or changed, over a period of 300–400 years!

You can find evidence of change by looking at the plan of a building or at the building itself. If you are looking at a *plan* look out for;

● evidence that the building changed or was added to,

● evidence about which parts where changed or added later,
● evidence about how long it took to finish the building.

If you are looking at *the building itself* look out for;

● evidence of different styles of building from different times,
● evidence of alterations, such as blocked up windows and doors,
● evidence about whether changes were wanted or needed.

Seenat and Joe have different answers to this question.

THERE WERE A LOT OF CHANGES IN THE MIDDLE AGES.

LIFE DIDN'T REALLY CHANGE IN THE MIDDLE AGES.

Conclusions: castles, cathedrals and the people of the Middle Ages

How did castles and cathedrals affect the people?

Castles and cathedrals changed a lot during the Middle Ages. The people who lived and prayed in them probably changed their ideas too. Think back to the story about Gudrun and Leofwin. What were their attitudes to these new buildings? Do you think that people's attitudes had changed by 1500?

At first, English people must have resented having new castles and cathedrals. These buildings reminded them that they had been conquered and the Normans had taken over. How would you have felt when a foreign army marched into your village? How would you have felt to be surrounded by soldiers speaking a different language? Many houses were pulled down to make room for Norman buildings. Domesday Book tells us that '166 were destroyed because of the castle' in Lincoln alone. The English also had to help feed the soldiers and pay for the buildings. In addition, some of the English saints' days were not celebrated in the cathedrals.

But attitudes probably changed. After a few years, maybe ten or twenty, young people would not remember life in England before the Normans. They had new churches and cathedrals to worship God in and often the new buildings were the largest centres for employment – cooks, stewards and stablehands were always needed. Do you think the youngsters would feel as angry as their parents?

However, castles and cathedrals were also centres of government. The sheriffs, barons and bishops collected taxes to be sent to the king and held court to punish crimes like theft or cutting down trees in the forest. This helped keep law and order but people may have had mixed feelings about this aspect of castle and cathedral life.

Later in the Middle Ages people became very proud of their cathedrals. Castles also gave some security. Bands of outlaws and robbers weren't likely to attack a village when castle soldiers were nearby. In the borders, castles gave protection from Scots, Welsh or French raiders. By 1500 people felt at home in their cathedrals and even in their castles.

This model gives you some idea of the scene when the Normans took over an English village. How do you think the English and Normans felt about each other?

((๑)) The king's visit

Ann and William ran out of the doorway but their father was already striding ahead of them, up towards the castle.

'Come on you two' he shouted. 'We've got to be there for first light. The steward's giving his orders then. So don't make me late. I'm not losing my job because you were hungry'.

So the children caught up with him and half walked and half ran up the hill. The king was coming to visit. Yes, the king. That was the excitement. And everyone wanted to help.

When they got to the castle gate they saw that the courtyard was already crowded, even though it still wasn't light.

'Women to the kitchen' shouted the steward. 'You men. Shift that waggon. You there ...' William stopped when his father set off to work in the stable. Perhaps he could do something important. Perhaps they'd let him serve wine at the king's table, or run messages or ... A slap from the steward brought William back to earth.

'We've no time for daydreaming, boy. We need water from the well. That will soon wake you up'.

Ann saw the look on William's face and laughed. It wouldn't be much fun for her working in the kitchen but at least it was dry and warm, with plenty to eat — not cold and wet like William's job. But Ann had only just got through the door when she saw one of the cooks signalling to her.

'Herbs. The fresh herbs' the cook shouted. 'We didn't have enough in the castle garden so my sister, Cecily, collected some extra ones for me. You know her, Ann. She lives beyond the town wall. Quickly. I must have them for the sauces. Wrap them in this napkin. Don't bruise them. But be quick. Run as fast as you can'.

Ann was out of the door before the cook could choose someone else. She ran across the courtyard, dodging the horses and waggons and barrels and then past the gatehouse and down through the town. The castle was so busy she'd forgotten how early it was. But she was in luck. The watchmen were just opening the town gate as she arrived. She squeezed through and hurried down the road and then out across the fields.

As she got near to the woods she saw that Cecily was busy milking her goat. Ann stopped long enough to collect the herbs, wrap them in the napkin and have a mouthful of whey and then she was ready again. But as she started back she caught sight of something struggling in the bushes. Moving closer she could see it was a hunting bird. It had leather thongs on its legs.

'That must be the lord's gyrfalcon' thought Ann, surprised. 'Father said that they'd lost it yesterday while they were hunting. I can take it back along with the herbs'.

But catching the falcon was no easy task. Everytime she got near, the bird lashed out with its claws or pecked at her with its sharp beak. In the end she emptied the herbs on to the ground, threw the napkin over the bird and then bundled it under her arm.

When she got back to the castle everyone was busier than ever. First Ann went to the stables and gave her father the falcon. He fetched its hood and soon had the bird settled on his gloved hand.

'Well done, lass' he called as he hurried off to the Great Hall. 'The lord will surely be pleased with you. This is his favourite. But get back to your chores now. The king's still more important than any bird'.

So Ann headed off to the kitchen to find the cook. William was standing nearby when she opened the door and she heard him laughing when the cook told her off.

'Don't bruise the herbs, I said. Didn't you listen to me girl? I gave you a napkin to wrap the herbs in. But instead you've bundled them up in your skirt. Didn't you listen to me?'

It was all sorted out in the end. Ann explained it all to the cook and then her father came in and explained it all again. And he was right. The lord was pleased. So pleased, in fact, that he allowed Ann to stand quietly in a doorway and watch the banquet. She saw the king and his lords and ladies — it was a wonderful evening.

For the rest of her life, Ann could remember about the time that the king came to visit their castle. But William never said much about it at all. He ended up turning the roasting spit in the kitchen for what seemed like hours. It was a horrible job. It made him hot and thirsty and burning fat kept spitting at him. And worst of all, he never got to see the king — but his sister did!

(@) From Gudrun to Ann

Like the story at the beginning of this book, the central characters aren't real. We have no record of William or Ann or their father. But the setting hasn't been invented. In 1487 King Henry VII visited Pontefract Castle, and people like William and Ann had to prepare for his visit.

PEOPLE IN THE PAST: LIFE IN THE CASTLES

1 How was life in a castle around 1500
   a different from your life today?
   b similar to your life today?
2 Was life in a castle the same in 1500 as it had been in 1100? Explain your answer.
3 Compare this story with the one at the beginning of the book. Did the families have the same attitude to castles?
4 Why were their attitudes the same or different?
5 Would you have liked to live in a castle? Explain your answer.

(9) What do castles and cathedrals tell us about medieval life?

Castles and cathedrals were needed for a variety of reasons – warfare, conquest, religion, homes, government

Life could be comfortable for people who were rich. Everyone liked colour and brightness

How would you describe life in the Middle Ages?

Medieval people were intelligent and skilful

Many things changed, like the design of castles. Some things stayed the same, like the importance of religion

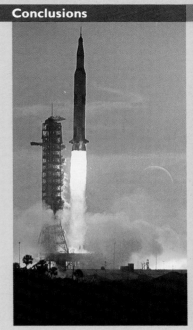

Today we're used to seeing skyscrapers and other huge, grand buildings, so a cathedral seems quite ordinary. But in medieval times a cathedral was very different from other buildings. Completing a cathedral was as remarkable then as sending men to the moon is today.

On page 6 you were asked to answer five questions. Each chapter has helped to improve your hypotheses. Now you probably have answers like the ones in the diagram above – but what about Question 5? This is your chance to give your final answer! You can use all the information on this page and it may help you to think about these ideas.

● What do castles and cathedrals tell us about medieval life?

● Are there any parts of medieval life that castles and cathedrals do not tell us about?

● What kind of activity today would be as spectacular as building a castle and cathedral in the Middle Ages?

● When you visit a castle or cathedral can you imagine planning and organising the building work?

Liverpool Cathedral was begun in the late 1800's but it still took almost 100 years to finish, partly because the two world wars interrupted the work.

Index

Oxford University Press,
Walton Street, Oxford OX2 6DP

Oxford New York Toronto
Delhi Bombay Calcutta Madras
Karachi Petaling Jaya Singapore
Hong Kong Tokyo Nairobi
Dar es Salaam Cape Town
Melbourne Auckland

and associated companies in
Berlin Ibadan

Oxford is a trademark of
Oxford University Press

Typeset by MS Filmsetting
Limited, Frome, Somerset
Printed in Hong Kong

👀 Notes to teachers

Exercises offering opportunities for developing
pupils' understanding of concepts and skills
required in Attainment Targets are signposted as
follows. Most (but not all) of the questions in
these exercises are linked to Statements of
Attainment. Here and throughout the book we
felt that remorseless linking of questions to
Attainment Targets would be an intolerable
burden for everyone. However, questions at the
end of each chapter do open up opportunities
for explicit discussion of the concepts that lie
behind the Attainment Targets. Such explicit
discussion is vital for the development of pupils'
understanding.

AT1a	Changes	15 35 43
AT1b	Causes and	
	Consequences	8 11 15
AT1c	People in the Past	46
AT2	Different Views	43
AT3	Evidence	19 25

Patricia Dawson   Ian Dawson